Soul You Vol. II

THE PROCREATOR

Soul You, Vol. II: The Procreator. Copyright 2021 by Sherika Frazier Duncan. All rights reserved. No part of this publication may be reproduced, distributed, or transmitted in any form or by any means, including photocopying, recording, or other electronic or mechanical methods, without the prior written permission of the publisher, except in the case of brief quotations embodied in critical reviews and certain other noncommercial uses permitted by copyright law. For permission requests, write to the publisher, addressed "Attention: Permissions Coordinator," 3819 Ulmer Court, Tallahassee, FL 32311.

Sherika Duncan books may be purchased for educational, business or sales promotional use. For information, please email the Sales Department at sales@sherikaduncan.com.

First Edition Printed, February 2021
Library of Congress Cataloging-in-Publication Data has been applied for.
ISBN: 978-1-7364355-1-9

CONTENTS

About becoming a woman 3

Herbs Importance 5

Herstory 11

    The Warrior Queen Amanishakheto or Amanishaket 11

    Isis or Aset 12

    Queen Heterpheres 13

    Queen Cleopatra 15

    Queen Candace Amanirenas 16

Ultimate Egyptian pharaoh 17

    Hatshepsut 17

    Queen Nefertiti 19

    Inari Kunate 20

    Queen Amina 21

    Queen Idia 23

    Queen Nzingha Mbande 24

    Queen Pokou 25

Saartjie "Sarah" Baartman 27

J. Marion Sims 28

Queen Yaa Asantewaa 31

Queen Nandi 32

Queen of Sheba 33

King Ahebi Ugbabe 35

Mary Bowser 36

Claudette Colvin 37

Henrietta Lacks 39

Dr. Mary McLeod Bethune 40

Dr. Frances Welsing 41

The mother of civilization is the producer of all offsprings.

Our purpose is to cultivate and motivate others with the possibilities, willingness to desire more while broadening their minds and nurturing their vulnerabilities, reminding them of their internal strength. No nation can rise without the rise of a woman; 75% of the work is with the woman;

There's no if, about it, we will free our sons because as a woman we rule the world.

These books are based on the reader's consciousness level to gravitate and build more curiosity about life and our purpose found inside this material.

Dedicated to my purpose,
Nia Janae Duncan,
with love.

Perception is critical because our gut gives us intuitive clues. Our physical eyes are only to interpret light traveling to our optical nerve visual cortex, transforming electrical coding to provide information on what we are visually experiencing. Sometimes, when we see objects, we may only perceive minimal observations, then someone else perceiving the same things may translate into an advanced interpretation. It is how we evaluate each other's level of consciousness.

Ancient storytelling allows us to grow to know of deity. We idealize personifications and naturally externalize these deities or energetic beings. Our thoughtform is so powerful with believing in something externally so much we create and give life and becomes real as an aspect of ourselves. Where we put all our energy makes the thoughtform and provides the thought with actual life. Yet its essence is meant to guide we internally, not materialize the entity instead of filtering the message through our ideas by connecting their experiences. There is a war on how we are internal.

We are all energetic beings magnetically attracted to figuring out the inner thought about the essence of deity. We can strategically allow us to see our level of consciousness by visualizing ourselves as these ancient essences. Our constructs require specific densified reality within the separated spectrum of light, flesh, and various chakras. Our destiny is to fulfill our life with purposefulness, love, happiness, and abundance. We purposely eat specific foods to have a particular result. We should be mindful of the things we externalize internally. We should organize our thoughts and be aware of the worlds we create internally or the external consciousness thoughtforms such as the practice of artificial intelligence. We must have control of the worlds we create internally, which may also appear externally. Repetitive things are often stored in our subconsciousness, such as tying our shoes, riding our bike, and how to drive a vehicle. Our mind should only utilize to learn and grow as within, so without so make sure we use how we operate in this world.

Commitment to Ourselves

Our commitment to self is to understand our value.
Our commitment to self is to know our worth.
Our commitment to self is to identify our usefulness.
Our commitment to self is to embrace our uniqueness.
Our commitment to self is to know our motivation.
Our commitment to evaluate is our level of self-fulfillment.
Our commitment to never under-value is our invaluable skillset.
Our commitment to reset our price when
deemed is necessary as we excel.
We are beneficial.
We are useful.
We are unique.

Commitment to Others

Our commitment to identify who are the people that need my talents and services.
Our commitment to aid and assist those who value also need us.
Our commitment to categorize the individuals who genuinely support our direction in life.
Our commitment to know the people who support our ideas.
Our commitment to understanding our place today to align ourselves in the right respected environments.

Soul You Vol. II: The Procreator

ABOUT BECOMING A WOMAN

Our Temperament

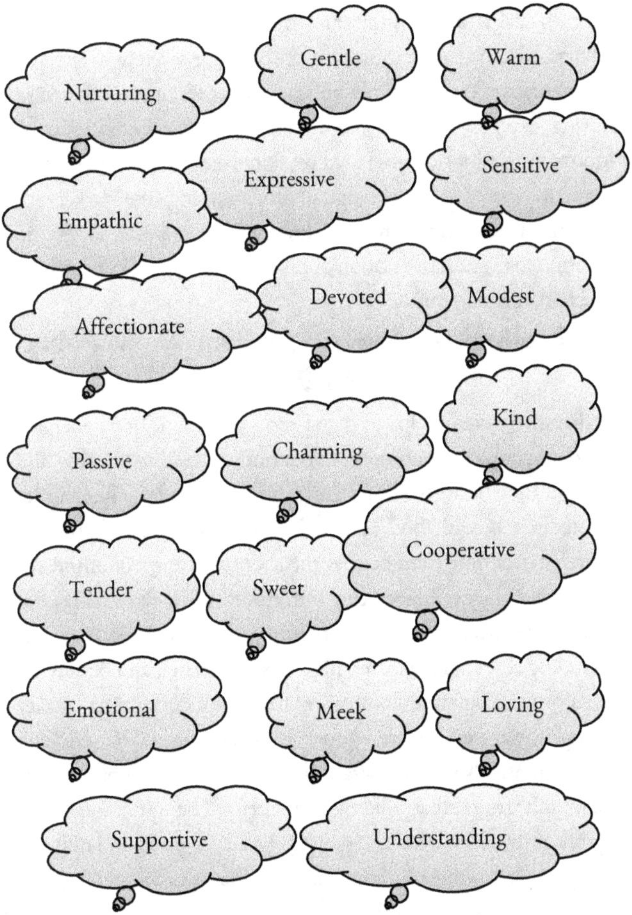

- Nurturing
- Gentle
- Warm
- Expressive
- Sensitive
- Empathic
- Devoted
- Modest
- Affectionate
- Kind
- Passive
- Charming
- Cooperative
- Tender
- Sweet
- Emotional
- Meek
- Loving
- Supportive
- Understanding

How to tap into our femininity?
Ever imagine how we are around infants and children?

Colorism is a pervasive system of inequality that negatively affects psychosocial and economic outcomes among African American adults. African American women and girls are severely affected by the pigment of our skin tone. This is proven over time subliminally, during slavery where African Americans were selected to work indoor or outdoor chores based on skin tone, which correlated to attractiveness. The psychological programming, the darker our melanin, the less attractive and lower-class we are to society, in addition to the negative notion of possessing an angry, irate attitude due to darker skin tone.

We are the first to show our families healthy eating habits.

A digestive system helps to digest food sources of body energies. Digesting improve every area of your body. Food preservatives and Bad gut bacteria are the cause. It is not hereditary; it is poor choices of traditional soul food habits. Our nutrition has significantly changed over time from healthy metabolism eating from the earth until enslavement. Since being introduced to a western diet of at least three meals consisting of farm animal, hybridized foods including cow milk, diabetes, high blood pressure, and obesity, to transforming our minds to eating to live by consuming quality spring water, fresh organic seeded fruits and vegetables reducing proportions. Also, for breakfast, the girls drank significantly more milk and fruits than did the women. The girls consumed significantly more bread and grains, vegetables, meat, and milk for lunch than women. For dinner, the women consumed substantially more bread and grains.

HERBS IMPORTANCE

Herbs derived from the land. It is a live source to provide healing to our bodies, hormones, and wombs. Herbs consist of weeds, shrubs, bark, flowers, and roots. The herbs possess savory sweet-smelling traits for healing purposes or aroma that help stop and control heart disease, cancer, and diabetes and flavoring foods. The pleasant gift assists with reducing or eradicating blood clots while giving powerful anti-tumor and anti-inflammatory properties. There are ongoing studies on herbs dating back to ancient times to use in tinctures and teas for medical health benefits. Garlic, linseed, fenugreek, and lemongrass may help lower cholesterol.

This Photo by Unknown Author is licensed under CC BY

Sherika Duncan

Are men intimidated by us? Because...

We are successful in the workplace or business.
We are more educated with more achievements.
We make more money.
We may come across as zero tolerance.
We shouldn't dumb down to appease him.

Things we can change.

Mean mugging, we can sometimes look difficult with an attitude. Our energy must feel relaxed, full of peace from within. How are we coming across? Are we exuding the energy that attracts the kind of men we desire? Maybe we are looking unapproachable.

We give off too much masculine *energy* we are operating in our workforce persona. A lot of masculinity exists in the workplace, so when we come home, we forget to turn the switch off becomes a problem.

Hiding behind the positive labels of strong women, successful women, and giving off evil energies.

Does it take a strong man to be with a strong woman?

No great men have options. Why deal with someone that comes across as problematic in a very negative way.

Let's look at ourselves in the mirror and check our spirit.

How are we coming across?

Are we being a difficult person that even other woman doesn't like being around?

Dating & State of Man
All adult males are men.
The man is categorized into categories describing the man's attributes can be immature or responsible.

What would we allow?
how many times will we allow him to come back?
Cheat in peace
hall pass
Has he created a riff to cause the break on a break?

How do we know if men love us?

They will be consistent in their actions and valuable to us.

Men will not pressure us to do what we don't want to do. Because They will be patient with us; They want to make sure we both are on the same page.

They are willing to listen to us. If not, men become very dismissive, impatient, unwilling to sit there, listen to us or talk to us.

We are here for their convenience. Men will embrace how we feel and listen to us mentally and emotionally. They will try to be in tune, hear what we are saying, understand it, and implement change. They are serious about us likely do love us trying to work with us to make things better—no time to listen to hear us out. Stay away from him; if we can't talk to our men, what's the point. We must learn how to speak to them. Our tongue is deadly. The way we speak makes people not want to sit there and engage with us. We should try to listen and be effective in our communication.

Men will push us to be our best selves. Perception: when people love, they will accept. Because we see flaws or things, we need to be improved. We push them to be better. We want to see the best out of them in hopes of experiencing a higher quality of life. God calls us to be more. He wants us to operate at a higher level. He will embrace us wherever we are, yet it doesn't mean He wants us to stay idle.

Do we look at the men we love and say, just stay where you are?

1. Men want us to be our better selves to get healing and find a passion in our life to reach that next level; that's what love does.

Do we tell our men it's ok that they're broke and have an attitude problem?

Instead, we encourage them and say we hope they will be better and inspire them to be the very best. Besides, we should desire to be better for our men. So, we may look good for them because we should expect to want to step up. Love will inspire us to be better.

2. Men would want to provide to us not financially but beyond money. Making sure we are right by pouring into us to ensure we have what we need. If Men are unstable, they shouldn't be in a relationship. They desire to find ways to still be an asset to us by taking the burden off our backs. Love drives them to do for us and give self-less.

If our men give money and nothing else, how is that love?
Men are providers who genuinely want to do for us.

1. Men will show us off when they are proud to have that woman. Men want to bring to their family or close friends around us. Social media is not a measure of someone's love. If they can't introduce us to family and friends, there is a red flag. If they think they have a toxic environment, but he is serious about us and truly loves us, they will show us off.

2. They will be willing to make sacrifices to get on the same page to find a resolution and make peace harmony in the relationship. We know our men are serious about us when they are flexible for the betterment of the relationship.

3. Anybody can do a good thing every so often. But our men will be consistent. Serious men will show us good healthy behavior by listening, sacrificing, and providing for us.

We must show appreciation when it's working.

Is it producing a good positive result? If we get a bouquet and don't display a genuine reaction to them, they will stop buying flowers. We are naturally expressive, so when we lack expression or appreciation, it translates into not being valued, so why should our men continue? If he stops, we may interpret it as games, but did we express how much we appreciated it? We must say it was necessary and valued their actions to express appreciation for our men's consistency. A reward is required when our men choose to do an act of kindness for us. As opposed to us thinking that's what men are supposed to do mindset.

4. If they are believers, men will pray for our best interest and happiness, peace, etc. The power of prayer is the most vital action we can do for someone.

5. We need to know how to be wives to great men like this.

6. Insecurity is triggered because we don't love the black man we are supposed to possess. We will treasure our black men as designed too.

7. Men's most crucial question is *who are we sexing?*

8. Use our thoughts to create our reality with emotion attached

HERSTORY

Nubia the land of the bow
The Warrior Queen Amanishakheto or Amanishaket
The Real Wonder Woman

The Nubian Queen **Amanishakheto or Amanishaket** succeeding Queen Amanirenas known as the warrior and ruler of the Nubian kingdom of Meroë from 10 BCE to 1 CE. Queen Amanirenas led troops with her bow in hand. Wonder Woman She had a son named Natakamani, who would later succeed his mother as ruler of Meroë. Archaeologists have uncovered female burials with essential grave goods, which provide some insight into women's importance. Women were viewed as givers of life, and in many cases, experts in agriculture. Nubian women also held an important role in religious rituals. Their role was vital in practices related to birth (creation), fertility, death, and rebirth.

Isis or Aset

Fact or Myth

She was a very influential deity in ancient Egypt and through the Roman Empire. She was adorned everywhere from England to Afghanistan. She is still revered by pagans today. It was said her primary focus was mostly griever because of her connection to corpses. She became a pillar in the community. **Isis or Aset** was known as a beautiful woman with a cow's horn on top of her head. Her husband was Osiris.

Queen Heterpheres

An influential mother figure named **Queen Heterpheres** in the old kingdom had a son Pharaoh Khufu. The Egyptians built elaborate tombs Pyramid of Giza pharaoh Khufu. In Egypt, Death was a transition to the afterlife when the soul will be reborn. In 1925, her enormous pyramid tomb chamber was found filled with gold at the room's deepest bottom. Heterpheres royal burial ever found all the contents relocated to Cairo museum including the bedroom suite silver headdress gold thrones and gold-covered boxes and unique collection of jewels silver bangles different size 4.5 thousand years old. She was the mother of King Khufu, being carried around by men in a carrying chair. She was far too important to walk across the grounds.

Lesson Learned:

_____
_____
_____
_____
_____
_____
_____
_____
_____
_____

Queen Cleopatra

In 69 B.C., **Cleopatra** came from a royal family. At the age of eighteen, her father was King Ptolemy XII, who died, which led to her and her brother ascended to the throne. After his death, Cleopatra and her brother's relationship became strained. She had to endure the struggle of overthrowing her only brother with the help of Julius Caesar of Rome and an army to defeat him in the Battle of the Nile. During Rome's civil war, Cleopatra and Julius Caesar of Rome became close after seeking refuge in Egypt. The two had conceived a son named Caesarion. Caesar was assassinated, then Cleopatra had a passionate love affair and fell in love with Marc Antony. In 30 B.C., she passed away from an Egyptian cobra snake bit. Thereafter, Marc Antony reportedly received misinformation about Cleopatra's death in an Actium battle, which led to him committing suicide. The two corpses were buried together, and Egypt became a province of the Roman Empire.

Queen Candace Amanirenas

332 BC, **Aminiras** became blind in one eye Queen Candace Amanirenas due to losing in a battle to King Alexander the Great with Romans attempted to conquer her land. Queen Candace exuded tremendous masculine energy. He decided to withdraw and head to Egypt instead. The feud between Alexander and candace's encounter was legendary.
Acts 8:27 refers to the Kush Queen.

Ultimate Egyptian pharaoh
Hatshepsut

She was one of the first fifteen women who ruled Egypt as a King or Pharaoh. As a talented builder and prosperous trader, Hatshepsut was in power for an estimated twenty years during the New Kingdom period. As the most successful female Pharaoh of ancient Egypt, they made a sculpture for her temple between 1479 and 1458 BC.

Lesson Learned:

_____

_____

_____

_____

_____

_____

_____

_____

_____

_____

Soul You Vol. II: The Procreator

Queen Nefertiti

Segenenre Tao and Ahhotep I are the parents of, Queen of the 18th dynasty, **Nefertit**i. King Ahmose married her before he was on the throne. Her health was fading fast. She was sick. 24th year of his reign, she died. Nefertiti was Ahmose's personal support system for everything. She even cheered him on as he executed his opponent while bashing his head in. Her tomb is in the queens' valley, very restricted, covering five hundred square feet journey into the afterlife high maintenance woman. In the company of Thoth god of knowledge and literacy and writing wing of the heart from the book of the dead, she said I am a scribe. She had writers to write on her behalf. Nefertiti had one son named King Amenhotep I. Ahmose-Nefertiti was deified after her death. The Queen was revered as "Goddess of Resurrection" and was arguably the most venerated woman in Egyptian history. She was a beautiful woman.

Inari Kunate

Inari Kunate was one of four wives of Mansa Musa. She traveled with Mansa Musa and took gold and five hundred maids-in-waiting during the famous journey. In West Africa, wearing gold, a scarce and valuable material, demonstrates power, prestige, taste, and fashion. Inari was the custodian of such values in her creativity with fashion and jewelry. Inari was not only the most beautiful of the four wives but also his favorite. She loved to swim each evening with her ladies-in-waiting at an a-special place in tie Niger, which flowed through her husband's kingdom. Every night after dinner, Mansa Musa would spend some time sitting and talking with her. Mansa Musa was always thoughtful, ensuring she was comfortable on the trip. Inari only missed her time swimming. One night he pressed her to talk about it more, and it was then that she confessed that she forgot one thing which would make the experience unforgettable. She missed very, very much her nightly swim in the Niger. Mansa Musa was concerned and decided to build a swimming pool for his wife in the middle of the Sahara. The other wives were impressed that Mansa Musa could respond so creatively to his favorite wife's wishes.

Queen Amina

Zaria, a major city in Nigeria family was rich in salt, horses. **Amina** sharpened her military skills as a fierce warrior. She acquired great wealth. Most men didn't feel threatened when women ruled in a position of authority. During the fall of shanghai 15th and 16th century Amina achieved dominance thirty-four years reign, leading a twenty thousand men army. She brought wealth to the kingdom with gold, slaves, and agriculture. Amina refused to marry anyone in fear of losing her right to power. Legends tell us, Amina did not allow a man to live to see the next day by death after being intimate. She is remembered for building the Zaria wall.

Lesson Learned:

_____

_____

_____

_____

_____

_____

_____

_____

_____

Queen Idia

[This Photo](#) by Unknown Author is licensed under [CC BY-SA](#)

In 1504 1550, **Queen Idia**, the rise and reign, left behind two powerful sons, Esigie and Obo, king of the Edo people. Idia received the credit of victory and medicine knowledge of Esigie's success on the battlefield for the kingdom of Benin.

Queen Nzingha Mbande

Nzingha Mbande was born into the ruling family Queen of the Ndongo, Nzinga. As a child, she received training in politics and the military. She is the Queen of Ambundu Kingdoms of Ndongo and Matamba, located in present-day northern Angola. Queen Mbande had demonstrated defusing political crises as the ambassador to the Portuguese Empire. In 1620-1660, there was a war with the Portuguese. Queen Mbande became the negotiator for communicating her central policy to conflict the port to the Congo with the Portuguese. As a result, she developed a profitable lasting relationship with the Portuguese by forming an alliance with foreign slave traders. Her treaty was highly smart with the Portuguese. She was known for maintaining peace and providing inspiration to her into her death.

Queen Pokou

1700 1720 **Queen Abla Pokou** was in the Ashanti kingdom of Ghana and was Nyakou Kosiamoa's daughter and the great King Osei Tutu's niece. After King Osei Tutu's death, Dakon, the brother of Abla Pokou, took reign. Abla Pokou was born into royalty. There is a strong parallel between Moses and the Hebrews in the bible. He led in their exodus out of Egypt. Like the Hebrews followed by the pharaoh's armies, Pokou's followers were pursued by Kwissi's soldiers. In the westward part of the Comoé River, they had fought panthers, giant ants, and giant snakes. Sometimes they crossed savannas filled with aggressive elephants, and serpents seemed always to lie in wait no matter what the terrain, while illness also dogged their footsteps. After many months, still pursued by Kwissi's troops, they reached the Comoé Riverbanks. Faced with a raging torrent, with no shallow fords or places for canoes to cross, Pokou and her followers decided that a sacrifice must be made to the river spirits. At first, their leader considered sacrificing a sick woman and her baby. She and the crew attempted to cross a raging river, but they were face death. Without shedding a tear, she threw her son into the dangerous river.

Lesson Learned:

_____
_____
_____
_____
_____
_____
_____
_____
_____

Saartjie "Sarah" Baartman

In 1789, **Saartjie "Sarah" Baartman** was a Khoikhoi native-born in South Africa's Eastern Cape. Her mother died when she was two years, and her father passed away during her teenage years. She belonged to the cattle herding Gonaquasub group. Eventually, Sarah married a Khoikhoi native drummer and had one son together who died at birth. At sixteen, her husband was killed by Dutch colonists. She was referred to as "Hottentot Venus." She was kidnapped and sold arrived in London. Scientists sought to learn more about her anatomical and physiological features by dissecting her private part. Sarah was referred to as a freak. They proclaimed to treated Sarah with the utmost kindness, providing her with a fair share of the profits in a state of coercion.

J. Marion Sims

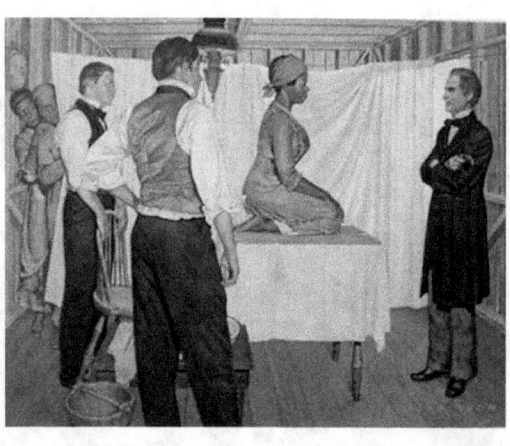

In 1837 in Montgomery, Sims developed his surgical expertise and techniques for treating cleft palate through enslaved African American women. Sims received permission to perform experimental surgeries specifically on three enslaved women, **Lucy, Betsey, and Anarcha**, and others, for four years. Drugs were used to keep the enslaved black women immobile and addicted to opium. There are statues and memorials of Sims for his accomplishments. At seventeen, Anarcha was in labor for three days, and Sims used his technique with forceps to complete her delivery. Afterward, she suffered from Vesicovaginal Fistula. In 1849, there were thirty surgeries performed without any anesthesia. He kept performing surgeries on enslaved Black women – to keep them fit to work and reproduce, not heal them. In 2018, due to the much-needed controversy over his methods, the City of New York relocated a monument of him, Central Park, to his burial at Brooklyn's Green-Wood Cemetery. **Frances Anne Kemble**

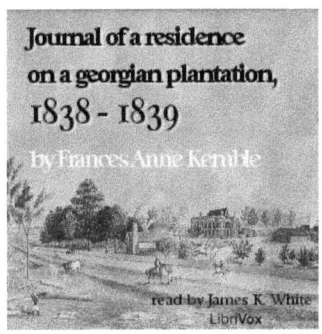

During the American Civil War in 1838-1839, **Frances Anne Kemble**, a Caucasian divorced woman of a slave owner, published a journal about the anti-slavery in a Georgian Plantation residence. His grandfather made him the heir to the cotton, tobacco, and rice plantations in Darien, Georgia. He became the slave owner to hundreds of slaves. He would always avoid taking Frances Anne and their children to the plantations during the early years of their marriage. After Frances's persistence, they finally visited during the winter of 1838–1839. Frances was very fascinated by her observations and wrote about them in a diary.

Lesson Learned:

_____

_____

_____

_____

_____

_____

_____

_____

_____

QUEEN YAA ASANTEWAA

Asantewaa was a very influential queen mother and powerful image. In Ghana 1880s, her brother, powerful ruler Nana Akwasi Afrane Okpase, appointed her to the role. Asantewaa became assigned as the gatekeeper of the golden stool, which represented the Ashanti kingdom. Queen Yaa Asantewaa was the 2nd highest ruler in the empire. The British attempted to steal the Golden stool from the Ashanti empire and removed the King and other Ashanti leaders. When the men wouldn't defend the people, the woman would rise in strength and resilience by rallying her troops, referred to as the Yaa Asantewaa war of independence.

QUEEN NANDI

Queen Nandi gave birth to a son named Shaka Zulu, who was born out of wedlock. She was determined to instill quality values into her son by shaping him into the most outstanding leader. Her efforts were not in vain because Shaka became King which Queen Nandi had a great deal of influence on Shaka and the village. Because she was the overseer of the military. In twelve years, the kingdom began to grow and establish. Shaka Zulu held women in very high esteem. Queen Nandi was essential because of her powerful conviction. In 1887, Queen Nandi passed away, leaving Shaka in deep mourning.

QUEEN OF SHEBA

In 1900 BC, **Makeda or Bilqīs**, Ethiopian Queen of Sheba, an intelligent African majestic queen who visited King Solomon to verify his wisdom. According to the Bible, Makeda's objective was to test King Solomon's wisdom by asking him to solve a series of riddles. Queen of Sheba was portrayed as interested in the great king of Israel spices, precious gold stones. There were significant trade ties between ancient Israel and Arabia. She was a beautiful, powerful black woman. The king's jinn assumed the king would attempt to marry Bilqīs. in mischief, he informed the King Bilqīs had hairy legs and the hooves of an ass. Solomon had a glass floor installed in front of his throne and tricked her into believing it was water, lifted her skirts to cross it, and discovered that her legs were very hairy. Then Solomon ordered the jinn to make a queen depilatory. Queen Sheba stayed there for six months learning from Solomon. She was tricked by the king into his room on the last night of her stay, and she got pregnant. She went back to her kingdom, where she gave birth to Menilek.

Lesson Learned:

_____

_____

_____

_____

_____

_____

_____

_____

KING AHEBI UGBABE

Ahebi Ugbabe was the only female King of Nigeria.
She possessed many roles as a slave, prostitute, wife of a deity, runaway, powerful chief. King Ahebi Ugbabe served as a collaborator to assist the British colony in conquering her village. Her independence helped to redefined sex work in Igbo culture. She traded Uganda into a business. King Ahebi Ugbabe was the only one in her village who can communicate with a Caucasian man and her town. Many Nigerians grew tired of her rules as King Ahebi Ugbabe received bribes. In 1946, she performed her own funeral because she didn't trust her society to properly bid her farewell two years before her death.

Takeaway - importance of our image

MARY BOWSER

Mary Bowser was a slave to the Elizabeth Van Lew family. She became a renowned abolitionist who freed slaves owned by the Elizabeth Van Lew family with her mother's help. Mary had a close relationship with the Van Lew family, which lead to her eventually becoming a spy, which infiltrate the Confederate White House. She received her formal education from the north then later traveled to Liberia to begin missionary work. In 1861, Mary married a servant named Wilson of the Van Lew family. A few days after their marriage, a Civil War started to erupt. Mary decided to help by supplying food, clothes, hidden messages, and even escape. She worked for President Jefferson Davis as a full-time cook and servant in the white confederate house. Later, Mary became a freed slave educator while traveling the country sharing her daring adventures as a spy.

CLAUDETTE COLVIN

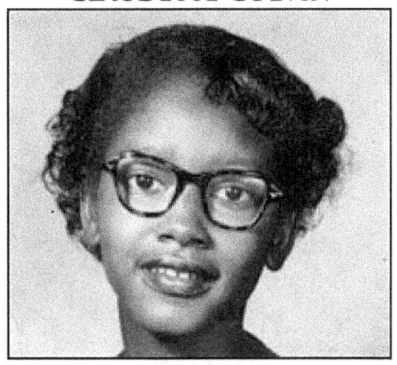

Very few know of Claudette Colvin's bus boycott dated nine months before Rosa Parks less peacefully. Claudette was fifteen years of age. We are all made aware of Rosa Parks' courageous bus boycott in Montgomery, Alabama. But other women were penalized with fines for refusing their seats on the same bus company. On March 2, 1955, Colvin, who now lives in Bronx, New York, recalls getting on the bus from high school, and the driver demanded her to move from her seat. The driver reported to the police, and two officers placed Colvin in handcuffs.

Lesson Learned:

_____

_____

_____

_____

_____

_____

_____

_____

HENRIETTA LACKS

In 1951, **Henrietta Lacks**, a five-year-old mother, died from her terminal illness with cervical cancer. Without Henrietta's consent, a surgeon named Howard Jones illegally extracted a tissue biopsy of Henrietta's cancerous womb shared it with George Otto Gey, a physician and cancer researcher in the same Baltimore hospital. Henrietta's Experiment on the HeLa cell line had a significant impact on medical science. HeLa is an immortal human cell line of durable and prolific cells gathered from Henrietta's cervical cancer treatment by George Gey, a Johns Hopkins researcher. Henrietta's cells were shared and multiplied in a lab setting. HeLa cells were transferred free of charge because they didn't' sell or profit from the distribution. They were stunned how her live cells were replicating in the lab due to cancer cells typically divides a few days then die off before any further studies could be done with them. In Henrietta's instance, they were immortally dividing with the necessary mix of nutrients for them to develop. Henrietta Lacks Family attorney conducted research to determine Johns Hopkins University denying making profits from the cells and never secured a patent. Yet, there are 17,000 U.S. patents involving HeLa cells that are making money.

Sherika Duncan

DR. MARY MCLEOD BETHUNE

In 1875, **Mary McLeod Bethune** was born in Mayesville, South Carolina, to Samuel and Patsy McLeod. Before the Civil war, her father was granted freedom from slavery. Then after Samuel McLeod saved funds in hopes of his wife from her slave master. Born into slavery, Mary was the fifteenth of seventeen children. Mary was interested in learning how to read and write. In 1894, she obtained a scholarship to Dwight Moody's Institute for Home and Foreign Missions in Chicago. Mary relocated to Sumpter, South Carolina, to attend Presbyterian Board to Kendell Institute. It is there where she met a former teacher named Albertus Bethune. In 1898, she and her husband had a son, Albertus McLeod Bethune Jr.

She relocated to Daytona, Florida, and started her own school on a dumpsite for a total of the five-dollar deposit and five bucks a month. In 1923, Mary's school transitioned into Cookman Institute, a school for boys. The merged schools became known as Bethune-Cookman College. She is the first Black to be recognized with a monument in Washington, D.C., at a Lincoln park to remind us all her outstanding achievements.

DR. FRANCES WELSING

Frances Luella Cress Welsing was the daughter of Dr. Henry N. Cress, a physician, and Ida Mae Griffen, a teacher, on March 8, 1935. In 1957, Dr. Welsing received her undergraduate degree from Antioch College and then attended Howard University in 1982, earning her M.D. She became an associate professor for her amateur Howard University while living in Washington D.C. She also was employed at several hospitals, particularly children's hospitals. In 1969, Dr. Welsing wrote and self-published her first book, "The Cress Theory of Color-Confrontation." Later in 1992, she released The Isis Papers: The Keys to the Colors. It was a compilation of thoughts through collective essays for over eighteen years. Dr. Welsing provided her perspectives on people of color concerning the global genocide and other challenges people of color experience. Dr. Welsing stated it is derived from the absence of Caucasians producing melanin. Her belief is when people of color acknowledge and understand, then openly dialogue the genocidal dynamic. Also, there is a need to find solutions for drug use, crime-related deaths, imprisonment, wealth, and infant mortality issues. Dr. Welsing strongly advocated the prevention of procreating black people is caused by the emasculation of black men.

Lesson Learned:

_____

_____

_____

_____

_____

_____

_____

_____

Survival mode

Dr. Frances Welsing instilled we must understand the moves
Caucasians make to ensure our survival on how to counter
the actions that can checkmate the opponent and move on to
victory. We must understand and the global minority
Caucasian motive.

Shades of Color

If you are black, stay back.
Brown stick around
Yellow, you're mellow.
Your white, you're around.
Rest in peace to all the queens in this publication.
It is truly a snapshot of so many others that came before us.

Heal the Land Procreators!

References

https://pubmed.ncbi.nlm.nih.gov/11928882/
https://journals.sagepub.com/doi/abs/10.1177/0095798420928194?journalCode=jbpa
https://files.eric.ed.gov/fulltext/ED132089.pdf
Tom Corson-Knowles - powered by FeedBurner
https://www.cdc.gov/vaccinesafety/ensuringsafety/monitoring/vaers/access-VAERS-data.html
https://vaers.hhs.gov/data.html
https://www.metmuseum.org/about-the-met/curatorial-departments/egyptian-art/temple-of-dendur-50/nubia
https://theafricanhistory.com/1242
https://atlantablackstar.com/2015/09/08/amanishakheto-warrior-queen-of-nubia-6-fascinating-facts-you-may-not-know/
https://www.britannica.com/topic/Isis-Egyptian-goddess
https://www.britannica.com/biography/Hatshepsut
eLimu | Great Queens & Kings of Africa (e-limu.org)
https://nazcargadwritersblock.com/queen-amina/
https://youtu.be/NuIJsGkV2h4
https://commons.wikimedia.org/wiki/File:Berber_Trade_with_Timbuktu_1300s.jpg
https://face2faceafrica.com/article/yaa-asantewaa-speech
https://neptuneprime.com.ng/2020/10/ahebi-ugbabe-prostitute-who-became-nigerias-only-female-king-during-colonial-era/
https://blackopinion.co.za/2016/12/17/queen-nzinga-brilliant-legacy-decolonization/

https://theafricanhistory.com/609
https://theafricanhistory.com/1259
https://theafricanhistory.com/1232
https://www.thekraal.co/history/queenablapokou
https://mnyamane.tumblr.com/post/145402125329/im-currently-reading-up-on-queen-nandi-ka-bhebhe/amp
https://blackexcellence.com/the-black-spy-that-infiltrated-the-confederate-white-house/
https://www.cookman.edu/about_BCU/history/our_founder.html

LEAVE A REVIEW AND PURCHASE OTHER BOOKS DIRECTLY ON WWW.SHERIKADUNCAN.COM

THE SETUP NOVEL

SOUL YOU BOOK COLLECTION
Soul You, Vol I: The Grand Awakening
Soul You, Vol. II: The Procreator
Soul You, Vol III: The Protector
Soul You, Vol. IV: Scribble Journal

media@sherikaduncan.com

Copyright © 2021 Sherika Duncan Enterprise

All rights reserved.

www.ingramcontent.com/pod-product-compliance
Lightning Source LLC
Chambersburg PA
CBHW062205100526
44589CB00014B/1961